Soundtrack to Your Next Panic Attack

Soundtrack to Your Next Panic Attack

Poems by

Mike Bove

© 2024 Mike Bove. All rights reserved.
This material may not be reproduced in any form, published,
reprinted, recorded, performed, broadcast,
rewritten or redistributed without
the explicit permission of Mike Bove.
All such actions are strictly prohibited by law.

Cover design by Shay Culligan
Cover image *#1460* by Bill Schulz

ISBN: 978-1-63980-496-2

Kelsay Books
502 South 1040 East, A-119
American Fork, Utah 84003
Kelsaybooks.com

for Andrew

Approach the night with caution.
You will know it's for the best
once tomorrow's morning quells
the thumping in your chest.

—*Evening Song;* Anastasio/Herman/Marshall

Acknowledgments

My thanks to the following institutions and publications in which versions of these poems first appeared:

The Café Review: "A Curious Feeling"

Deep Water (Maine Sunday Telegram): "In an Email from Kevin," "Piano"

Hole in the Head Review: "The Million Dollar Bridge," "Scene from Last Thursday"

Main Street Rag: "In Bed at Nine on a Weekend"

The Maine Review: "Basho's Death Poem, New York City"

Poetry East: "In Praise of the Humans at Gate A18," "Mother Pattern"

Slouching Beast: "Rats Live on No Evil Star"

Writing the Land: "Sanctuary," "We Always Need"

Several generous writer friends helped in various ways with this book. I thank them all: Ken Craft, Judy Kaber, Melissa McKinstry, Jefferson Navicky, Bill Schulz, David Stankiewicz, Meghan Sterling, Kevin Sweeney, and Erik Wilbur.

Contents

Prelude

Basho's Death Poem: New York City	17
In Bed at Nine on a Weekend	19
The Million Dollar Bridge	21
In Evergreen Cemetery	23
St. Peter's Italian Bazaar	24
A Note about the Streets in Portland, Maine	25
Five Points on My Father's Map	27
As We Age We Resemble Trees	30
Without Moving	31

Overture

Family Wedding	35
Love & Shame	36
Cul de Sac	37
Something Held	38
Together Waving	39
Brother Music	40
Piano	41
Crossing the 45th Parallel at Daybreak	42
Hymn for the Downtrodden	43
Learning to Walk	44
Water from Stone	45
The Father	46
A Curious Feeling	47
Last Coffee	48
Whose Woods	49
Listen	50
Time Moves through Us	52
Sanctuary	53
You Asked What Teaching Is Like	55
Ursa: Major & Minor	56
When Ice Melts	57

Fugue

Mother Pattern	61
Redolence	62
This Is What It Means	63
Kind Neighbors	65
Little Bob	66
Rochester Good	68
What Happened at the Cemetery	69
Denouement	70
Spring Cleanup	71
A Note about Weight	72
My Mother's Liturgy	73
Talking to Nate at the Funeral Home	74
Whale Fall	75

Crescendo

To Margaret Fuller as Her Ship Goes Down	79
Eden	81
To the Student Who Shot His Mother	82
Rats Live on No Evil Star	83
To the Future	85
No One Told You	86

Coda

We Always Need	91
Scene from Last Thursday	92
Warm Night, Mid-April	93
Consider the Multiverse	94
About Marriage	95
In Praise of the Humans at Gate A18	96
In an Email from Kevin	97

Prelude

Basho's Death Poem: New York City

Sick on a journey
my dreams wander
the withered fields
        —Basho

In an old notebook were the beginnings
of a poem about Basho's last poem, the one
he composed while he died. In the notes,
the speaker walks from 31st Street to 17th
in Manhattan and remembers Basho's lines.
He is visiting the city in summer with his brother
who has stayed in the hotel, tired of the heat.
The notes say this, and the first line
of the would-be poem is: *Walking hot streets,*
I think of Basho. The poem wants to follow
the speaker as he passes kabob carts
and a group of college kids with clipboards
soliciting signatures. The notes say that the poem
should quote Basho's death poem like a refrain,
that the speaker should be made to feel
momentarily sick, or lost, walking unfamiliar
streets in the heat, hungry for a journey
he didn't know he wanted. Every time
the speaker steps he thinks of his brother
napping in the cool hotel room and Basho's dreams
in the field, wandering. All of this is in the notes.
But really the speaker is nothing like Basho,
and death is incomparable to a hot city walk, so
the unwritten poem gets it wrong, and Basho's
death poem stays singular and unparalleled,
while the speaker of the non-poem keeps walking
through Union Square Park and on toward
the Lower East Side. No end to the walking because
the notes won't make it into a poem.

Distance increases, the speaker moves off
the map and disappears into the East River, the heat
becomes unbearable, and the brother continues
dozing, oblivious and satisfied with
non-existence in a wandering dream.

In Bed at Nine on a Weekend

The neighbor's kid is high again,
sitting in his car belting
the refrain to some howling rock song.

The song's not bad, but you can't tell
who it is, and the app on your phone
that solves such problems

isn't working. You hold it up in the dark
of your bedroom, your wife beside you.
If she wants to know what you're doing,

she's too tired to ask. Last night, in the city,
you saw streets filled with young people,
their skin so smooth and trim-fitting.

When it started to rain, they huddled
in doorways and hugged themselves,
bare-armed and gorgeous.

You never thought you'd be middle-
aged. You never thought you'd say
young people. You never thought

you'd be in bed at nine on a weekend
trying to get your phone to recognize
the song the neighbor's kid

is butchering. And now your wife
is asleep, breathing low. And now
it begins to rain again, but instead

of getting up to close the windows,
you stay in bed, listening to it fall
against the roof, listening to your

wife's deep breaths and the primal
whine of the neighbor's kid, all
blending in accidental chorus

into something familiar but forgotten,
a song you used to sing and still could
if only you remembered the words.

The Million Dollar Bridge

The city does not remember itself
in decades past, poised on the cusp,

and the sailors and fishermen who
used to slip out of bars on Fore Street

find their living elsewhere now,
in care of their children or nurses.

I remember a downtown building
in demolition, empty and open in front.

At night, bright colored lights
fell on two life-sized dinosaurs,

Tyrannosaurus and Stegosaurus,
made of wood, possibly,

and covered with plaster and paint
by some upstart artist who

stuck them there so kids like me
would have something to marvel at

as they came over the bridge, the bridge
we called the Million Dollar Bridge,

though surely it cost more than that.
I can't tell if my memory of those dinosaurs

is real, and I know I said the city was
on the cusp, but a city is always

on the cusp, like the people
who call it home, endlessly shifting

in time with the dinosaurs
and the kid who loved them, in the car

with his parents coming over
the bridge, past waterfront bars, old

cobbled streets, and quiet fishermen
trapped in nets they crafted by hand.

In Evergreen Cemetery

Vandals toppled the headstones
of former residents of
the home for aged women.
Passersby saw boys running
from the area: a parcel of cemetery
shaded by centennial spruces
where the graves of women
from the 1850's go mostly unvisited.
Police have added patrols, but
the boys won't return. They've grown
into men who stay up late
looking out windows
unable to forget the sound of stone
falling heavy into earth.

St. Peter's Italian Bazaar

My father brought me to the bazaar
at St. Peter's, the street out front closed
to cars but open to vendors, games, raffle tables, all
to benefit the church his father, my grandfather,
helped establish a hundred years ago when Italian immigrants
were held in suspicion and permission for a church
was given on condition the entrance not face
Congress Street. A pole stood near the steps, de-flagged
and slathered with grease. For a dollar you could try
to reach the top for a prize, and a pair of older kids
hopped and slid, losing their grip, onlookers
cheering below. I didn't see anyone make it.
Thirty years later I brought my boys to the bazaar.
The flagpole was there and so were the young
bodies pushing toward the prize.
We stepped inside the open church to see
the stained-glass window bearing my grandfather's name,
a man I met only in stories, then back out
to the vendors and games and a small tent
where volunteers displayed scattered scraps
of church history. My grandfather stood
in a yellowed photo with other men under a label
asking: *can you identify anyone in this picture?*
Afterward we watched a trio of kids try the pole,
their hands slipping each time they gained, heaving
themselves and hoisting one another, slick feet
on shoulders, grunting, laughing, struggling, failing,
reminding me of when my father brought me
to the bazaar, my father now a story I tell
my boys along with stories about my grandfather
mixed with stories of other people walking into
and out of the church or trying the games, stories
told of men in old photos, stories told as they're lived,
retold, reached for and told again so we can hold on
a little longer, trying in the telling to keep them
from sliding away.

A Note about the Streets in Portland, Maine

Streets lie flat and face the sky.
If we were the same, we'd be
eternal star-gazers, hopes directed

ever upward. I drive the bridge,
take High Street to the square,
then down the hill to the park where

the unhoused gather, anchored to
the streets. When I'm on the highway,
the crumbling train trestle is over the water

farther out. There are plans to tear it
down. I heard a group of residents
wants to turn it into a path for walking.

My car doesn't know what streets it's on,
though it's driven them countless times,
and I only use their names if I'm telling

a story about where I was when I saw or
felt something. My son had a dream
about a terrible accident and the next

morning at dawn on her way to work,
my wife saw a car crushed in a median ditch,
hidden under a halved spruce. She called

the police, and first responders came.
She thought about checking on the driver, but
something held her and she was better for it:

he was dead and young and had been there
all night. I couldn't help, when she told me,
thinking about the streets. Washington Avenue,

Congress Street, Forest Avenue, Free Street,
Fore Street, Ray Street, Preble, India, others.
Despite what does or doesn't happen on them,

I love the streets, I love them and I'll
know them always because that's how to
love: know something forever like the streets

in Portland, Maine, edges and rough spots
and cracks and holes. Slopes, up or down,
asphalt tributaries unfixed in time, carrying

all of us who have ever travelled them,
living or dead, standing and walking or
flat on our backs watching the sky.

Five Points on My Father's Map

1.

My father's antique map hangs
on my bedroom wall. He found it
rolled and jammed in the eaves
of his parents' attic. No one told him
it was there. No X to mark the spot.
I turn in bed and stare each morning
at pencil-thin streets, boxed buildings
and angled churches. Sometimes
I see him by the waterfront
or in the tiny dark window of St. Peter's.
He disappears faster than I can say
I love you.

2.

The atlas I keep in the trunk
was his. He used it to mark
familiar routes and day trips
in highlighter with dates
inked beside them. A hike
to the tourmaline mine
with my brother and me
in '89. Trips to ocean trails
in '90 and '91. He didn't need
maps to find these places.
He was making his own.

3.

Wind doesn't blow on a map.
Rain doesn't fall.
I scratched directions
on the back of a receipt
before visiting my college girlfriend
for the first time. A three hour drive
from my campus to hers.
Halfway there it jumped
from my hand and out the window.
I stopped but didn't know where
to turn. It was getting dark. I found
the highway. I was late.
I was speeding when the trooper
pulled me over. I asked for directions
and went to a pay phone.
My father's response when I confessed
the ticket was the silence
I knew as disappointment.

4.

I was married four years
when my parents split.
My father kept the house
for a while, so I knew where
to find him. Inside those walls,
everything had changed.
Unfamiliar topography,
a dirt path I hadn't noticed before.
And his face folded wrong.
Later he sold the house
and found an apartment.
I quickly memorized the route.

5.

On the map in my bedroom, I show
my boys the street where my father
grew up. I show them the house
where he moved after the war. I show
them the street where I grew up, the street
where their mother and I had our first
house, and the street where we live
now. If they ever need to find me,
I say, follow the map. My youngest walks
his fingers between our house and where
my father lived. Between now and then,
time is lost in his small hand.

As We Age We Resemble Trees

And now we are adults
who were once frightened children

beneath layers of night,
making prayers in the dark

to a god we couldn't see: please
keep nightmares away,

no glow-eyed werewolves
at the bedroom door, no

brooding father in the study or
drunkspun mother down the hall,

please make daylight break
forever. In time we grew

alongside silent trees, thick,
twisting toward the instant

some years on when
we woke to a past, gone

but still noisy. Listen:
the world wants us here,

gnarled and writhing,
heartwood pulsing.

We are older and broken
and needed and worthy.

Without Moving

Mornings like this I prefer to stay in, out
of the rain. It's cold, even for June in Maine.

I putter through some drawers, find a photo
of my 8th grade science project (second place),

then some letters and cards from my dad, dead
four years ago this August. On each envelope

he sketched a playful sign that bore my name,
a flat plank on a post inked in black. He liked maps

and long roads, liked to plot a path. He saw signs
as spectral gifts from those who went before,

he knew *future* as another word for *past* with
signposts, locations on a map with *present*

in-between. I've been lost there before,
so it's good to see my name on signs

so I remember how to get around. The rain,
old photos, a father's paper voice:

if you've ever wondered how to travel
without moving, this is how it's done.

Overture

Family Wedding

Together we were like leaves:
autonomous forms
from a common root.
The wedding gave us time
to talk and laugh, retelling
the best stories,
and when the sun fell
behind the Rockies, we danced,
nothing between our bodies
but time and fondness.
The band played songs we knew.
The saxophonist climbed on a table
and leaned far back, blowing celebration
at the mountains. No one had to say
how good it was. Hours later,
tired and gathered in clusters,
we walked to the cars. We could still
hear the band as we slipped away
beneath separate stars and somewhere
along the road, party lights fading,
my youngest in the back, his
voice on the edge of sleep:
why do we always have to go
during the best songs?

Love & Shame

In time, winter's weight
always smothers summer's
thrusts of green.

Or is it the other way, where
light and warmth are the natural
easing of all icy burdens?
Can earthly things ever rest
between contentment
and desire?

              The clock face
glows, watchful in the night.
A deep breath from the dark side
of the bed tells me you've fallen
asleep.

Cul de Sac

what do they mean   screams

spilling from creatures

in the night   hunted or hunting

coyotes yowl

at the dark and dead end of the street

someone's cat gets a mouse

a raccoon raids the compost   in dreams

dead loved ones drift through

murky echos of places we know

and suburban night leaks in

while we sleep   a skunk lurks

near the garden   an owl scans

for twitches in the grass

we float to the window to examine

darkness   we flip a light

a singular glow in a row of lookalike boxes

sloping   toward the end

Something Held

Near the pond
behind the cemetery
I knelt
before my son
my hands
a cradle for his
where he kept a frog
before it leapt away
a ring of ripple
the only proof
it had been there
at all. He wept
at its absence
and I brought him to me
knowing
someday when
he was big
I'd remain
on my knees
mourning
that something held
and learning to let it go
only after
my hands were
empty.

Together Waving

Nights with fog invite surprise
like the one I moved through in 1995
with my first girlfriend
out on the point by the lighthouse
at the end of a breakwater
we couldn't see but knew was there.
We were alone
except for a man and two children who
stood on the seawall to watch
something large and luminous
move through the thick night.
We stopped some yards away
and saw it too, one of the cruise ships
that used to come and go
to and from Nova Scotia. Then flames,
little bursts, and two sparklers
for each child, waving and yelling
to the ship: *goodbye, goodbye mom*.
And far off, a flashing reply: *goodbye,
see you next week*. We'd stumbled
into someone else's intimacy
on our way through ours,
clumsy and stuttered, more important
than anything else,
even the future, dim and distant,
not mattering until just now:
the family on the seawall
lost to memory, my first girlfriend
gone with the decades,
all of us together
waving goodbye.

Brother Music

When my boys argue, I worry
someday they'll grow tired
of one another's noise, jabs
about table manners, stolen
socks: everyday cruelty
exchanged while mosh-pitting
from room to room. I want to
tell them their uncle and I never
fought, an outright lie, because
I remember well the hot rage
when your brother lands
a gut-punch dead on
or rats on you for sneaking
a cookie seconds before dinner.
Growing up with another
is hell, but wonderful and
short, and I hope my boys
are listening now. I hope
they see their uncle and me
meeting for meals or
going to see our favorite bands.
I hope they understand
someday when it gets quiet,
when the music stops,
they'll want a friend with
common history, someone
to walk home with
when the show is over.

Piano

After the gig, we loaded out
through a side door

and I saw the old upright
they'd left by the dumpster

to be hauled away.
We'd played new material

to an empty room
and I knew it needed work.

It was the deepest part
of February, so cold

ungloved hands could've
gone mute in minutes, but

something about a piano
waiting for its end got inside

deeper than chill. I reached
and rolled a trill of major notes

into the dark. It was nothing,
but it was enough

to curb the cold for a half-step
and might have been

the best thing
I played all night.

Crossing the 45th Parallel at Daybreak

cold inside the car   coiled

inside the mist   striking

oversized landscape of green

firs taller even than memory

the car whispers between trunks

like eden's serpent   ghosts

set to wailing and creatures rise

with the sun   this is temptation

to stop moving   within

a shaft of light   the forest closes

eyes   something stirs

ghosts return to sleep

coils tighten and release

Hymn for the Downtrodden

We must consider ourselves
fortunate to be
brutalized by existence.
So we are told,
trudging through
common back alleys
with the world
dangling from our necks.
We are lucky to be alive
in so glorious a place,
the rats at our feet
grinning their hardscrabble grins.
Yes, we are in love with it all
and yes, this day is a gift,
a sodden box
on the steps in the rain,
left by a distracted courier
rushing from house to house,
cold and dreaming of supper.

Learning to Walk

One odd step
in the ice storm
and you're soaring,
arms swinging
before collapsing in snow,
sleeves and collar filled,
hot pain at your hip.

Angry at your carelessness
you fill the night with curses
then pause, suddenly ashamed
you'd nearly forgotten
there are other selves
alive inside you,
one of them a child.

Water from Stone

Just once
you'd like to be water
dependent on churn
and satisfied to stir
for eternity
instead of the stone
thoughtlessly tossed
in the creek
by a quiet man
too busy to note
moonrise
over the distant city
where he was
born.

The Father

In one of these houses he tries
to sleep. Mice have arrived

in the attic. They etch sounds
in the dark and he is awake

not because of them but because
earlier, in Emily Dickinson's biography,

he learned what she wrote
about her father, *he never played,*

and though he does, he worries
he's doing it wrong. Maybe

he didn't learn to play correctly,
too focused on rules,

maybe that's why his boys
bring their problems to their mother,

their talks a poetry he fears
he'll never hear. Never

is too long to consider before
sleep, so he is awake,

doubts drifting like echoes,
or shadows, or small sounds

swelling to roars
at the tiny tip of a mouse's claw.

A Curious Feeling

My clothes are small. It happened overnight.
My wrists hang outside my cuffs in dangle.

I bring the dog outside, watch him leap
into the woods. Birds alight from the pines.

I must have expanded in the night as I thought of you.
When the dog comes back there is no wind.

I hope to be right-sized by noon.

Last Coffee

for A. H.

now that you're gone
what I think of most

is that last coffee before
you moved to Pittsburgh

then Kalamazoo
then Spokane

before your diagnosis
and chemo

and the letter I wrote
to your widow

about our last coffee
and the things

I wish I'd said while
people came and ordered

got into cars and drove away
and didn't see us

like we were ghosts
like we were never there

Whose Woods

We walk the path by the pond
to see six acres
recently up for sale.
The dog's nose
whispers above deer tracks.
How long until it will sell,
you want to know,
how many houses and where
will the road go?
There and there, I point,
and we see flags of neon tape
tied at intervals around young maples.
When I was your age
I was with friends
in the trees and one day
there were the same
little flags. We knew
our woods were lost.
We pulled them all down
anyway, in case there was a chance.
And now you see a flash of white.
And now four deer bounce out ahead.
And now the dog yelps and pulls.
You say you'll be sad
when the houses come,
and the road.
A red-tail appears and makes circles
over the pond.

Listen

My father calls to me
from the yard. He wants me

to stack wood, and after that,
cut the lawn. In his office

by the hospital, he says I can have
a donut from the box his nurse

brought in. He's across the street,
telling the neighbor what to do

about high blood pressure. He's in
his study at the old house, where

I'm on the couch with a stomachache
watching him at his desk. His pen

moves over paper and he knows I'll be
fine. *I need you,* I say, but he's not

quite listening; he's watching my boys
play little league and hooting when

they hit. He's sitting with his face in his
hands trying to decide if he should go

to assisted living. He's mumbling
and confused but cheerful as years

pass, one after another and another
until their passage removes all sound,

until suddenly he speaks the last words
I'll ever hear from him when I walk into

the ER the day he leaves for hospice,
when he turns to the nurse with a smile

and points to me: *look who it is!*

Time Moves through Us

Watch a moth
emerge at dusk
to hurl itself
moonward
before resting
in a field to die.
A tree gets big
and falls.
The dog you love
stops fetching.
One day you'll
slow down
enough for time
to pull up a chair
and won't you be
better for it
since only then
can the two of you
really talk.

Sanctuary

The paths I walked were
an amalgam, a spider's web
threading marsh and pine.

One summer, I discovered
something poking out of the water
in a marsh stream at low tide.

I don't remember descending
into mud, but soon I was shin-deep,
pulling at corroded metal to reveal

frame and footpeg, fender and wheel:
an abandoned motorcycle, hidden
for who knew how long or why.

I thought I could dislodge it
and get it home. My dad had the tools
and soon I'd ride the neighborhood

in triumph. But day was ending,
the tide was swelling and soon
I'd be lost to darkness and water.

I was so close. When it reached
my waist the sky was pink.
I remember letting go, watching

the bike get swallowed.
I promised I'd return, and I did,
though thirty years later

with my own boys, walking trails
until an accidental glance brought it
back in sharp surprise. Still there

at low tide: the motorcycle and me
pointing, thrill in my voice
as memory surfaced, spreading

a web of remembered days,
intricate as a spider's
in late-summer sun.

You Asked What Teaching Is Like

We give them hives
to turn and tilt
in search of
shifting sweetness.
Some of them can't
or won't
and split themselves
between
bitterness and boredom
but others
get stung by wonder
and meet a happiness
that expands
continues to swell
and some years on
when they're out
walking the dog
planting peppers
or dropping a friend
downtown
quivers inside
like a handful of wings.

Ursa: Major & Minor

for Dana Wilde

Two bears, big and small,
slide their starlit bulk in a circle
all year. In early stories,

celestial hunters stalk them
spring and summer. The bears
flee month to month until slain

in fall when their blood
becomes the changing leaves.
They death-sleep through winter

and are reborn only to be hunted
again. This is eternity. Standing below,
we have questions too large to voice.

The night sky redoubles
with enormity and we escape
inside, pursued by a bear.

When Ice Melts

This is the world we forgot
last fall. When winter

brought cover, we didn't care
about the disappearance

of fallen leaves, litter we never
collected, or tools left

on the porch. Snow took them
and we knew to accept it.

We slept for months until
rains came, bright sun

and ice-shells hatching
forgotten relics from before.

We didn't hide them on purpose
but we forgot, and forgetting is

a kind of hiding. When ice melts
they slowly emerge, a little worse

for wear. Oh, we say, there's
the handsaw, the electric bill

that blew off the stoop. There's
my former self emerging

from the crust, cold and stiff but
still in working condition.

Fugue

Mother Pattern

In better times
I liked to watch her
by the window in the evening
doing cross stitch
from patterns.
The clock ticked
evenly as dusk arrived.
Wouldn't it be nice,
I thought, if every night
was just this way.
Wouldn't it be nice
to know where
to pull the thread
and what was coming
next.

Redolence

We made decisions
in a small room
down the hall from where
our father lay dying.
It was summertime.
Outside, people mowed lawns.
We didn't remember
the plain white shirts
he wore mowing in summer,
but in the coming weeks
of cleaning out his things,
we'd find them,
pull the folds to our faces
and breathe.

This Is What It Means

        even much later
she can't understand either side of it—
        the feral urge to drive to empty places and drink
or the impulse to take the boy
though his father begged her not to—
        put him in the car—
        beyond reason—
        too drunk to hear
above the turning and swerving—
        a cemetery outside the city
where frenzied geese beaked divots into the fender—
        a dark hotel stairwell
where a startled janitor looked the other way—
        parking lots and dead ends—
        tearing through everyday streets
with the boy in the back where he held his eyes
on her hands loose on the wheel
afraid if he looked away she'd let go—
        the needle edging 60—
        deaf to his clipped breaths and prayers—
        she lurched to the curb—
        lumbered out—
        opened the trunk—
        pressed a bottle to her face and sucked it hollow
as if and because her life depended on it—
        even much later
she doesn't know he still sees
his own fists balled around the lap belt—
his mouth sealed silent
and the places she took him
and the position of the sun
and how it fell on passing cars—

      how could she know if no one does
what he remembers so clearly
though he can't understand both sides
of the memories or why they have two
or explain how he knows that this is what it means
to see a thing as if you've lived it twice—
      both a world away
and so violently right here

Kind Neighbors

With an open door they let him in
when his mom was sleeping it off
and the bus dropped him
at his house, too quiet, and he knew
that silence and was afraid to stay
and had learned to walk
to their house instead
where they'd be home because
they were older and retired
and gave him peanut butter cookies
and let him eat while they ducked
into the kitchen to call his dad at work
to say he was safe but his mom was
drunk again, and again he'd come
knocking at their house where
they smiled and thought they knew
what was happening though
he didn't, because he was five
and kindergarten only went
until noon and the only thing
that got him through was knowing
someone would be there when
he got out, not at his house
but at theirs, kind neighbors
who let him have cookies
and felt so sad and tried to help
and knew what was going on
but didn't know the half of it.

Little Bob

His emerald green Lincoln
was often parked out front,
flaps covering the headlights
like closed eyes. I wanted to know why
she called him *little*. She gulped
cold Folgers and smoked Marlboro Lights
while my father was at work. She said
it was because he *was* little
and there was already another Bob
at the club. She brought me with her
to the Sahara Club, named for a very dry
place, where meetings were
on the second floor and in the kitchen below
Little Bob cooked hot dogs for me while
she was upstairs. Sometimes I had
Pepsi. Sometimes she wept
on the drive home. My father
said Little Bob was her *sponsor*
in the *program* because she was *sick,*
words that were questions I didn't ask
and every night I couldn't sleep, awake
in bed listening for noise.
Sometimes she made Folgers
for Little Bob after I went to bed.
They smoked on the porch and played cards.
I guessed her sickness had to do
with what she drank and how much
and made her angry and made it hard
for her to walk and speak and sleep.
Sometimes she was up all night.
Sometimes by herself. Other times
with Little Bob, who talked
and smoked and played cards and stayed
until dawn, until she finally slept,

when he walked to his Lincoln
where it dozed in the driveway
and disappeared into the soft light
of a dry morning.

Rochester Good

After college there was Rochester, New Hampshire
and a sunlit second-floor apartment across from

the high school where the marching band botched
pop songs on a sun-scarred field every Saturday, down

the road from a Kmart, recently closed, a Blockbuster
Video, and an empty shoe factory. A local joke

claimed whenever anything weird or horrible
was reported in New England news, it happened

in Rochester. The man who robbed a bank wearing
a zebra suit: Rochester. The nun chased through

the convent yard by a rabid fox: Rochester.
When I asked the landlady where to eat, she named

her favorite place. When I asked if it was good, she said,
Rochester good, which meant just OK. For a year

I tried to live like nothing was chasing me. I was tired
but free. I met morning sun where it came through

the bedroom blinds. I listened to the band and forgave
their blunders. Nothing was weird or horrible.

I ate at the landlady's favorite restaurant, rented
the latest movies, watched the moon ascend

over the darkened shoe factory, and taught myself
to rest comfortably knowing something

was coming but unsure what it was, hoping
it would be better than just OK.

What Happened at the Cemetery

None of us knew what to do
once my father's ashes were in the ground
and my half brother, estranged
from the rest of us, took his turn
to leave a shovelful of earth on top
but seemed unable to stop, adding pile
over pile when the rest of us
had left just one, arms rigid in his blazer,
piercing and piling, until
a nod from my sister moved my nephew
to place a steady hand on his back
and lean in close to say,
that's probably
enough.

Denouement

I couldn't save you
from that brutality of omnipresence.

Newly married in our own place,
she drove by during dark hours, slowing

to look through the windows.
I learned not to pick up the phone

and returned from work to a machine
full of labored breathing.

What did she want, and why, when we
went out to eat, did we glimpse

her Toyota lurking on street corners,
striking away the instant we saw?

I used to pray when I was small, but
no one answered and I grew

uneasy with age, filled with shame
each time I saw you tremble at the window

where you peeked between the shade,
and every night, watched you

check and double-lock the door
in a doomed attempt to keep out

what had already gotten in.

Spring Cleanup

Small in the doorway, she
watches us clear knotweed
from the granite foundation of the barn
that burned with the farmhouse
when she was young. She can't do the work
herself, her arms and legs too loose
and shaky. Sober today, she's happy
to have her boys here.
The house she lives in was her parents',
built where fire took the other one,
with the barn, cow, a rusted tractor, and chickens.
The day gets long. Sunlight heats
foundation stones hauled from the field
generations ago. I ask if I can bring a few home
for the wall I'm making around my garden.
My brother and I work until evening
when she offers dinner, but I don't need
anything and we hug goodbye,
weedy growth cut back for another year.
I load the stones, we beep and wave.
I don't turn for a look at the foundation,
pale now and exposed. Instead I watch
my mother in the mirror, small
in the doorway, getting smaller.

A Note about Weight

If nothing holds us down, do we drift off
and quickly disappear? Afraid to find out,
I roamed the woods behind my house, filling
my pockets with stones. I watched my brother

climb our tree fort, then fall, folded
on a limb before he hit ground, breathless,
his mouth a great dark hole through which
no air would pass. Maybe something

weighed him down. Maybe he slipped
on a half-nailed step. Maybe I could have
caught him, if only I wasn't afraid to leave
the dirt, anchored by nerves and believing

my center of gravity must always be
the lowest possible point. I get smaller now,
a little shorter every year, heavy with panic
I keep in unseen pockets. *You've got to lose that*

weight, my brother says, breath restored,
a little at a time so you won't drift up too fast,
and together we learn to fall, gasp, to turn out
our pockets and use that emptiness to rise.

My Mother's Liturgy

Now I see her restraint
on sober days,
lining up for communion
at ten o'clock mass
following a homily
on Christ's time in the desert,
defying the call of a cup
brimmed with holy blood,
returning to the kneeler
with lowered eyes,
tongue splitting dry wafer
with a snap
she alone can feel
in a vast wilderness where
she sidesteps temptation,
momentarily ascendant.

Talking to Nate at the Funeral Home

We'd come to ask about
our father's remains
but more specifically
whether it would be ok
to put his ashes
in a vintage mason jar
one of many he'd collected
and Nate said sure
as long as we were ok
with the sight of ash
through the glass
and we said yes
that would be fine but
just to be certain
my brother asked
it'd only be ash right?
not a chip of tooth or
errant bone?
and Nate said gosh no
nothing like that
and there in the back room
by polished coffins
and a wall display of urns
we laughed at the question
as if it was silly
as if we were talking
about something silly
like a jar of lost buttons
or rainbow gumballs
and not the earthly flakes
of a human man
who taught us
boundless love.

Whale Fall

is when a whale
sinks to the seabed and dies

in the dark. Creatures come
from all directions

to nourish on what's left.
In turn they nourish others.

This can last fifty years.
This is how time works.

This is how I feel about love
when I think of my father,

left behind in stories like tides
bringing what I need

for the coming years, an ocean
of stories, waves of them,

big and small, even
the one I'm telling now.

Crescendo

To Margaret Fuller as Her Ship Goes Down

You're off the coast of Fire Island and your ship
hit a shoal or reef and your young son
is in your arms and your husband is there, or he's
your partner and you're not married,
the biographers aren't sure, but you've been
in Italy for years loving him and writing
and raising a child, which isn't something
you thought you wanted when you left Concord
where you walked with Emerson and rowed
with Thoreau—now hold on to that deck-rail
though it's soaked with rain, and hold on to
your child though the crewmen are yelling
to put him in the skiff, and search the sky
in all directions for light though you can't tell
which way is east, and cry, Margaret, you have to
cry, because you don't know how this ends
but we do—we know your ship goes down, we know
your little boy drowns, we know you
and your husband die and most of the crew,
and we know they'll never find your body
though pieces of the ship will wash ashore
and someone will recover some of your letters
but not the book you were finishing,
and people in town will catch wind of the wreck
and the items washed up and some of them
will come to the water to scavenge
for things to sell and Emerson will get
an urgent message and send Thoreau
to look for you and when he arrives
on the beach the ship will be gone and he'll see
a scattering of people going through
the wreckage and one of them will be
wearing your coat and he'll manage to

tear away a single brass button he'll hold
in his palm when the sky clears and the sun
strikes it creating a glint we'll remember forever
because we can see it all the way from here.

Eden

Apple seeds won't kill you, though they contain
amygdalin, a naturally occurring cyanide.
I'm sure my dad knew it and didn't think twice
about eating apples whole: core, stem, and seeds.
It was one curiosity of many, a trick, a quirk
that was further endearing as he aged, quieted, forgot
everything, and died. We chalked it up to
the Depression: he'd watched his parents lose
their house, their money, watched his father's clients pay
their bills with boxes of apples left on the doorstep.
That must be why he washed plastic baggies
and strands of floss, collected rubber bands and saved
week-old salad, edging brown. He told us over and over
the story of his mother hanging cheesecloth sacks
in the kitchen to make applesauce, squeezing
from the top to let the wet meal drain. We could see her,
though she was gone when we were born, see her
turn each apple as she peeled. It was a different story
of apples than the one we knew from church
of Eve felling humanity in the garden, or the one we saw
on screen of the gnarled witch bringing Snow White
to her knees. Apples are storied fruit, and not just because
of how my dad ate them. Fruit is metaphor
in Genesis and long before, in West African myth
and stories older than we can imagine. It's likely
my dad learned not to waste apples from his mother.
And Eve is our true savior; falling is really ascension
into living, tasting loss and knowing beauty
by way of pain. No one wants to live in Eden
where nothing happens and nobody knows
the sweetness of an apple; an offering
left on a doorstep in the dark, a talisman
we consume and absorb, a reminder of knowledge
gathered as we tour time, falling and rising again
and again, learning, like my dad and his mother,
that living is more pressing with poison on your tongue.

To the Student Who Shot His Mother

A colleague said he only hears about
past students when they've done something
terrible, so when I see your mugshot
in my morning feed I'm tempted
to go no further, but I remember you
as friendly and funny, always polite,
so I click a link that carries me through
the night you brought a hunting rifle
to your mother's kitchen where
she stood by the window and you fired
until the only sound was your frenzied breath
and the clatter of the gun as you let it slip
and the slosh of gasoline and flare
of the match when you tried to burn
the house, then the hum of your truck
on backroads where you drove
until noon when they pulled you over
and cuffed you and later, at the jail, when
they asked why, you said you just snapped,
and reading these things I knew
your happy, warm way was just one thin layer
above some dark scrim I might have pierced
if only I'd said the right thing
or gotten to know you better, so I wrote you
a letter, started it and stopped
over and over until I settled on talk of weather
and the seasons and said I imagined
you were lonely and kept it short
because what do you say to the student
who shot his mother except I'll never forget
your mugshot, those spectral eyes
and how young you looked,
and I'm sorry your mother is dead,
I'm sorry you killed her, but most of all,
more than anything, I'm sorry
I couldn't save you.

Rats Live on No Evil Star

It turned out they were eating birdseed
that fell from the feeders while
Cardinals and finches came and went.
We watched them slide out from under the deck
at dusk to collect all they could before
booking it to the woodpile.
So I took the feeders down, raked up
the fallen seed, thinking I could
drive them away with deprivation.
Four nights in a row that week
my son couldn't fall asleep, but it had nothing
to do with rats. He was anxious
and grew panicked as hours passed
and the rest of us slipped into dreams.
Fear must've fed itself as he waited in bed,
awake and alone night after night. I didn't know
what to do. I worked at understanding, which
usually came easy, but he was newly teenaged
and spent daylight hours muttering
and stomping off. More nights passed, days,
until one morning at the kitchen window
I saw a rat nosing the lawn where the seed
had been, searching in clear daylight,
tense and desperate. I called my son
to come with me and we snuck outside,
back around the house, but the rat
saw us and bolted. We split and jumped,
sudden herders, trying to keep it from
getting into the garage. No more than
ten seconds in all, our hearts beating fast
and his glorious howl when I shrieked
as the rat dove past my boot and disappeared
beneath the neighbor's fence. He tired himself

laughing but still couldn't fall asleep
that night, so I sat with him and told him
the longest palindrome I knew,
rats live on no evil star,
and told him to work it in his head
back and forth letter by letter until sleep came,
imagining kind rats, loving and loyal,
bounding through the ether on a celestial quest.
I don't think it solved anything; he still
had a hard time many nights after. But he
eventually did sleep that night, and so did I,
and days moved into weeks, punctuated
by usualness. Soon I put the feeders
back up, the finches and Cardinals happy
to have them, and though I know they were
still there, lurking in the night beneath
the sky's distant galaxies as my son struggled
to sleep, we never saw another rat.

To the Future

We don't have much time so we hope
you'll forgive the rough nature of this:

There are things we want to know before
you arrive and we need to know them

now. For instance, tell us about the ice.
Has it melted yet and if so

how much new water is there?
Enough that the creek near the house

has flooded the basement, outswelled itself
and taken away all homes for mice?

Are the cities lost? And what about
the forest paths we used to walk, and are we

so nervous still, are the kids OK, and
did we ever figure out how to fix

the upstairs faucet? Tell us all you can
about the clouds and how often it rains.

Are wildfires worse and what about the
food? How good are bagels and is the coffee

strong? There's so much more but we're
running short. We won't be here

when you arrive so we'd like to know
how to leave things, and more than that,

more than anything, we want to know
how best to love you.

No One Told You

No one tells you they grow up fast.
I mean, people say, *they grow up fast,*
but no one tells you what it means
or that it's easier when they're small,
when all you have to do is feed them,
clean them, snuggle, read, build forts,
position bandaids, and survive
without sleep when one wakes at four
for eight straight weeks and the other
refuses bed until midnight, collapsing
on the rug beside puzzle pieces
and crumbs. No one tells you
you'll think it couldn't get harder until
middle school, then high school, until
they start talking back or saying *fuck*
or keeping things from you.
Even then no one tells you how much
everything they do makes you
laugh, weep, yell, curse, and love them
harder than you thought possible.
No one tells you how often their questions
and fears, none of which you can answer
or allay, play in your head on repeat
like the soundtrack to your next panic attack,
and every night, in bed on your back
under a blurry moon, you'll map their lives,
prepping the journey, until finally
you fall asleep only to jump up moments later
and find nothing worked
like you thought, your plan was bullshit
and they've taken the wheel,
you're just a passenger whose job is to bring
snacks and gas money and when you break down

and pop the hood and start pulling at wires
and hoses and plugs, you'll have to figure it out
on your own, as you go, no manual,
trial and error, you'll have to make it work,
and you will, and despite the pain you'll want
nothing more or as much, and that's the point,
you're not in charge,
and that's what no one told you,
you got lucky enough to suffer this way
so enjoy it.

Coda

We Always Need

Pockets of natural light
and trees: coniferous/deciduous.

Places to walk that are far
from home. But not too far.

Rainwater, birchbark,
rolled stones, and air.

Paths made by
people before us.

Paths we made
ourselves.

Scene from Last Thursday

L texts from the dentist's to say C needs his wisdom teeth out, and my response is *wtf* because we just finished paying for his braces. Later at home L explains if he doesn't get them out all that work will be for nothing because the wisdom teeth could tear through and start screwing with the straight ones. But I've stopped paying attention and instead I'm wondering why they're called wisdom teeth, and why if they're so esteemed do we get them yanked, and does all that yanking incrementally decrease the world's level of wisdom or is it the other way around and the coffers of wisdom fill because we're smart enough to rip those suckers out before we're all walking around jaw-hacked and tooth-snaggled? *Who knows,* I say out loud and L looks at me funny which signals I've answered a question she hasn't asked which signals I wasn't listening and the eyes she makes tell me, in case I didn't know already, who is unwise.

Warm Night, Mid-April

In the reeds past the culvert,
green is coming.

The neighbor's porch light is on.
The peepers bring us

to sit at fires and think
of last year's passage.

Voices trail in the dark.
A dog barks.

Something rustles the old leaves
and we are still in love.

Consider the Multiverse

Some of us subscribe
to a theory of infinite universes
where familiar versions of ourselves
make alternate choices and live
differently. Could we rest a little
more comfortably believing
some cosmic doppelgänger
chose paisley over plaid,
or that the ugly impulse
of an unwise ancestor
didn't drag through our synapses
the moment we were born?
I could be tempted to exist
in another world entirely, but
really I'd rather remain in this one
where scattershot decisions wait
in dim winding hallways
and nothing makes sense
but you.

About Marriage

I want to tell you
it's like
those paintings by Vermeer
in the way the room stays
the same
but the scene is always
changing
filling with familiar people
some like ghosts
and children who start small
and get big
their height marked
on the north-facing wall
heartache hanging
in their absence
and while we're at it
let's acknowledge
little cruelties in corners
and the dark parts
near the edge
but the best thing is
the eye can't stay
long in those places
before it sweeps
to the left
and that big window
sometimes open
often closed
but always
filled with light.

In Praise of the Humans at Gate A18

Waiting in the Denver airport
I fall in love with everyone:
grandmothers playing crossword
on their phones,
men with beards and coffee,
the redheaded woman
in a stare-down with her laptop.
Wrappers crackle.
Clouds of conversation materialize
and disperse: *Did you check
the coffee maker? I think
we missed our gate. Hold this
for a sec.* Some of us claim
other people are intolerable,
and maybe that's true, but here
I'd like to hold on to everyone
for one warm moment
before boarding call,
before we rise and scatter
in unison, alone together.

In an Email from Kevin

I like walking
in places
      where
I can see houses
and especially enjoy,
when passing by
      at night,
the appearance of
      lights.

About the Author

Mike Bove is the author of three previous books of poems: *EYE* (Spuyten Duyvil, 2023), *House Museum* (Moon Pie Press, 2021), and *Big Little City* (Moon Pie Press, 2018). His work has appeared in journals in the US, UK, and Canada. He was winner of the 2021 Maine Postmark Poetry Contest and a 2023 finalist for a Maine Literary Award in poetry. He is Professor of English at Southern Maine Community College and lives with his family in Portland, Maine where he was born and raised.

www.ingramcontent.com/pod-product-compliance
Lightning Source LLC
Chambersburg PA
CBHW071010160426
43193CB00012B/1991